Horses and Ponies

Written by Cathy Jones
Reading consultants: Christopher Collier and Alan Howe,
Bath Spa University, UK

First published by Parragon in 2012

Parragon
Queen Street House
4 Queen Street
Bath BA1 1HE, UK

ISBN 978-1-4454-6651-4

Printed in China

Discovery KIDS™

Horses and Ponies

Bath · New York · Singapore · Hong Kong · Cologne · Delhi
Melbourne · Amsterdam · Johannesburg · Auckland · Shenzhen

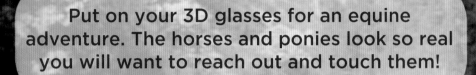

Put on your 3D glasses for an equine adventure. The horses and ponies look so real you will want to reach out and touch them!

Parents' notes

This book is part of a series of non-fiction books designed to appeal to children learning to read.

Each book has been developed with the help of educational experts.

At the end of the book is a quiz to help your child remember the information and the meanings of some of the words and sentences. Difficult words, which appear in bold in the book, can be found in the glossary at the back. There is also an index.

Contents

Horse or pony?

Horses and ponies both belong to the horse family. The difference between them is their size.

We measure horses and ponies in **hands**. One hand is about the width of a grown-up's hand.

Mane

Withers

Hoof

The area between a horse's shoulders is called its **withers**. We measure horses and ponies from the ground to their withers.

A horse stands at least 14.2 hands (5 feet) high. A pony is usually less than 14.2 hands high.

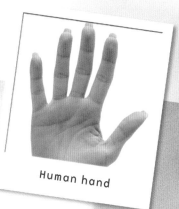

Human hand

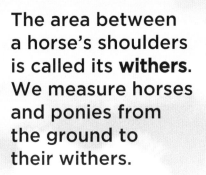

Tail

DISCOVERY FACT™

Thumbelina is the smallest horse in the world. She is just over 4 hands high. She only comes up to an adult's knee.

Shapes and sizes

Horses and ponies come in many shapes and sizes. The different types are called **breeds**.

Suffolk punch

DISCOVERY FACT™

Horses wear metal shoes to protect their feet. Some people think a horseshoe is lucky.

The Suffolk punch is a giant of the horse world. Its size and strength make it ideal for heavy farm work.

An Arabian horse is smart and fast, and has a good nature.

The little Shetland pony is a good size for small children to ride.

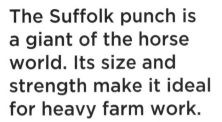

Arabian horse

Shetland pony

A gray is usually born black, bay, or chestnut. After birth the coat color changes.

Colors

Horses come in many colors. Their coats may also have patches, spots, or white markings on them.

A horse with a white coat is called a gray.

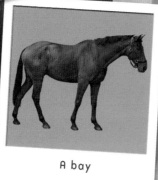

A gray

We call a horse with a black coat, mane, and tail a black.

A chestnut has a red coat, mane, and tail.

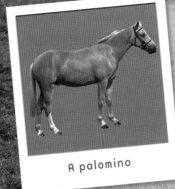

A bay

A horse with a brown coat, black mane, and black tail is called a bay.

A palomino has a golden coat, with a silvery mane and tail.

A palomino

Family life

Male and female horses have babies called foals. The male horse is the father of the foal and the female horse is its mother. Most foals are born in the spring.

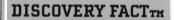

DISCOVERY FACT™

Foals get their first teeth at one week old. Human babies have to wait about six months.

A male horse is called a stallion. Stallions will fight to protect their mares.

A female horse, or mare, carries her foal inside her for 11 months.

At first, foals feed on milk from their mother. Soon they are grazing, or eating grass, just like their parents.

Mare and foal

Living wild

All over the world there are horses in the wild. Many have no owners. They live in groups called **herds**. Each herd has one stallion and a few mares and foals.

New Forest wild pony

There are herds of wild ponies in the New Forest, England. They often search for food in tourist campsites!

Mustangs live in the western United States of America. Some live in the cold mountains. Others live in the dry deserts.

The brumby lives wild in parts of Australia. It is thought of as a pest by some humans, but others try to protect it.

Brumby

Przewalski's wild horse, which lives in Mongolia, has never been tamed by people.

Mustangs

Taking good care

Horses and ponies need good food and exercise. They must be brushed, cleaned, and combed. In cold weather they need the shelter of a warm stable.

Brushing and cleaning is called grooming.

In the field, horses and ponies eat grass. Indoors, they need hay three times a day.

Horses and ponies always need fresh drinking water. The straw, or bedding, on the stable floor needs changing every day.

Grooming

Changing the straw

DISCOVERY FACT™

A horse has a frog in its foot! The soft part of a hoof is called a frog. Always clean it with care.

Working horses

People and horses have always worked together. In the past, there were no tractors or trucks. Even today, people still need horses for work.

A horse is fixed to a cart with a **harness** and padded collar.

In colder countries horses are used to pull sleighs on snow.

Horse and sleigh

19

Saddle

Stirrups

Ready to ride

Getting on a horse is called mounting. When you have mounted, you sit up straight, put your feet in the **stirrups**, and hold the **reins**.

The equipment that your horse wears is called the **tack**.

The horse has a metal bar called a **bit** between its teeth. It is fixed to the reins. To control the horse, you pull gently on the reins.

Bit

Reins

Riding helmet and gloves

A hard helmet protects your head. Riding gloves and boots protect your hands and feet.

DISCOVERY FACT™

You can braid a pony's mane and tail for an extra-special look!

Riding

Horses and ponies can move at four different speeds, called **paces**. Different paces are used for different jobs.

Riders use their hands, legs, and bodies to control their horses. They pull softly on the reins and gently squeeze the horse's sides.

A walk is the horse's slowest pace. Each foot goes forward in turn.

Walk

A trot is faster. The rider rises up and down in the saddle.

Trot

For a canter, the rider sits firmly in the saddle.

A gallop is a horse's fastest pace. Horses gallop in races.

Canter

When a horse or pony gallops, all four feet come off the ground together.

Gallop

Show jumping

Horse sports

Horse sports have always been popular. We use horses in all kinds of games and competitions.

In show jumping events, horses and riders jump over fences.

Rodeo

In the sport of **rodeo**, cowboys ride with and without saddles.

Polo

Polo is the fastest ball sport in the world.

DISCOVERY FACT™

In the sport of horse-racing, riders are called jockeys.

Quiz

Now try this quiz!
All the answers can be
found in this book.

What is the difference
between horses
and ponies?

a) Horses are brown and
ponies are black
b) Horses are larger
than ponies
c) You can't ride a horse

What color is
a bay horse?

a) Brown
b) Red
c) Black

What is a baby
horse called?

a) A pup
b) A foal
c) A kid

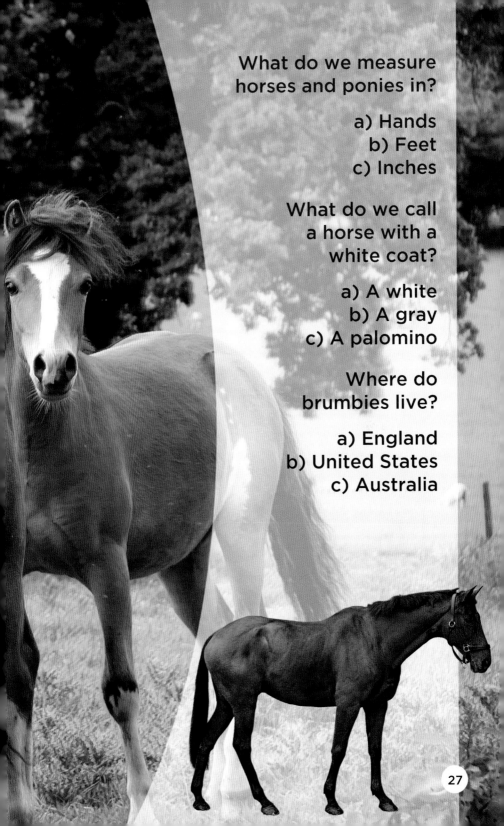

What do we measure
horses and ponies in?

a) Hands
b) Feet
c) Inches

What do we call
a horse with a
white coat?

a) A white
b) A gray
c) A palomino

Where do
brumbies live?

a) England
b) United States
c) Australia

Glossary

Bit   The bar we put in a horse's mouth that helps a rider control it.

Breed   A type of horse or pony. Each type has certain qualities, such as speed or strength.

Hand   The measurement we use to work out a horse's height. One hand is about 4 inches.

Harness   The straps a horse wears to fix it to a cart.

Herd   A group of horses that live together.

Paces   A horse's movements—a walk, trot, canter, or gallop. Each pace has its own beat as the horse's hooves touch the ground.

Reins   The straps for a rider to hold.

Rodeo   A competition where cowboys show off their horse riding and cattle handling.

Stirrups   The two metal loops where riders rest their feet.

Tack   The bridle and saddle.

Withers   The area between a horse's shoulders.

Index

Acknowledgments

t=top, c=center, b=bottom, r=right, l=left

Cover: All images iStockphoto

p.1 Ivan Tykhyi/iStockphoto; p.3 Ivan Tykhyi/ iStockphoto; p.4–5 David Gomez/iStockphoto; p.6–7 Bob Langrish, p.7tr Marc Dietrich/ iStockphoto, p.7b Brad Barket/Getty; p.8–9 Bob Langrish, p.9tl/tr Horsepix; p.10–11 TheBiggles/ iStockphoto, p.10tl Kit Houghton/Corbis, p.11tl/ml/ bl Horsepix; p.12–13 Agnieszka Pastuszak-Maksim/ iStockphoto, p.12tl Hlavkom/Dreamstime.com, p.13tr Terry W. Eggers/Corbis; p.14–15 Catherine Karnow/Corbis, p.14tr AtWaG/iStockphoto, p.14br Samantha Coates, p.15tr Frans Lanting/ Corbis; p.16–17 benoit jacquelin/iStockphoto; p.18–19 Jan Tyler/iStockphoto, p.19tr Corbis, p.19br jim pruitt/iStockphoto; p.20–21 Loretta Hostettler/iStockphoto, p.21bl Terry W. Eggers/ Corbis; p.22–23 Perkus/iStockphoto; p.24–25 Andre Gravel/iStockphoto, p.25tl Robert Y. Ono/Corbis, p.25cl moodboard/Corbis, p.25bl Neil Farrin/JAI/Corbis; p.26–27 Eileen Groome/iStockphoto, p.27b Horsepix

Additional images used on sticker sheet: iStockphoto